# ENGAGING SOCIAL-EMOTIONAL SKITS FOR

# GIFTED STUDENTS

T0372236

*Engaging Social-Emotional Skits for Gifted Students* gives you all the tools you need to help gifted children expand social skills and develop a better understanding of self, peer relations, task commitment, and leadership through insightful, engaging roleplay!

Presented in an easy-to-read, conversational style using real-world examples, these open-ended roleplay scenarios teach students how to recognize, monitor, and adjust their behavior. Covering topics from anxiety to patience to teasing and cooperation, each skit includes a problem that invites students to develop their own solutions and takeaways from the situation.

Ideal for learners in grades 2–6, these skits allow gifted students to engage with social-emotional learning, making tackling difficult social and emotional issues nonthreatening and fun.

**Laurie Stolmack Eaton** has over 30 years' experience working with gifted and highly gifted students in grades K–12. She has previously served as a gifted and talented teacher as well as a specialist with the Denver Public Schools Gifted and Talented Department.

# ENGAGING SOCIAL-EMOTIONAL SKITS FOR

# GIFTED STUDENTS

## Prompts and Roleplays for Grades 2–6

Laurie Stolmack Eaton

Routledge
Taylor & Francis Group

NEW YORK AND LONDON

**ENGAGING SOCIAL-EMOTIONAL SKITS FOR**

# GIFTED
# STUDENTS

First published 2022
by Routledge
605 Third Avenue, New York, NY 10158

and by Routledge
2 Park Square, Milton Park, Abingdon, Oxon, OX14 4RN

*Routledge is an imprint of the Taylor & Francis Group, an informa business*

*Library of Congress Cataloging-in-Publication Data*
Names: Eaton, Laurie Stolmack, author.
Title: Engaging social-emotional skits for gifted students : prompts and roleplays for
   grades 2-6 / Laurie Stolmack Eaton.
Description: New York, NY : Routledge, 2022.
Identifiers: LCCN 2021046998 (print) | LCCN 2021046999 (ebook) | ISBN 9781032206349
   (hardback) | ISBN 9781032206271 (paperback) | ISBN 9781003264491 (ebook)
Subjects: LCSH: Gifted children—Education (Elementary) | Gifted children—Education—
   Psychological aspects. | Affective education. | Simulation games in education. | Role playing.
Classification: LCC LC3993.22 .E37 2022 (print) | LCC LC3993.22 (ebook) | DDC 371.95—dc23/
   eng/20211025
LC record available at https://lccn.loc.gov/2021046998
LC ebook record available at https://lccn.loc.gov/2021046999

ISBN: 978-1-032-20634-9 (hbk)
ISBN: 978-1-032-20627-1 (pbk)
ISBN: 978-1-003-26449-1 (ebk)

DOI: 10.4324/9781003264491

Typeset in Helvetica
by Apex CoVantage, LLC

# Contents

## Peer Relations Skits        46

# ENGAGING SOCIAL-EMOTIONAL SKITS FOR
# GIFTED STUDENTS

# Introduction

"*That's me! That's me too!*" a gifted second grader states in response to two successive scenarios regarding "Knowing Yourself."

"*That really happened to me*," a sixth grader confides after working through a "Peer Pressure" skit.

*Engaging Social-Emotional Skits for Gifted Students: Prompts and Roleplays for Grades 2–6* is designed to help gifted children expand social skills, improve leadership skills, and develop a better understanding of self, task commitment, and peer relations. The skits in this book are presented in an easy-to-read conversational style, using real-world examples to teach students how to recognize, monitor, and adjust their behavior.

## Here's How It Works

Students are put into small groups. The skit begins with a stated topic (i.e. Knowing Yourself), a given scenario (i.e. perfectionism), and opening lines. It is then up to the students to develop, and act out, appropriate ways to handle the given situation. The skit ends with a final thought for the scenario.

As a longtime gifted teacher and specialist, I have used these skits with students in grades 2 through 6 with positive results. Whether in a character education group or a classroom setting, these skits help make tackling difficult social and emotional issues nonthreatening and fun.

# Teacher Directions

1. Select a prompt from a specific social-emotional focus area.

2. Divide students into groups of two or three and give the chosen prompt to each group.

3. Instruct students to select roles.

4. Students complete the script (orally or in writing) and perform an example of an appropriate way to handle the situation. The skit ends with a final thought for the given scenario.

5. After each group presents their skit, discuss similarities, differences, and solutions to the problems addressed.

6. Give students opportunities to share personal experiences pertaining to the given prompt (whole group or one-on-one).

7. You may want to save student skits for future roleplay (tackling reoccurring issues and celebrating successes).

# Additional Ideas

- Give different prompts within the same topic area. For example, if your topic is "Peer Pressure," each group could perform a different peer pressure prompt.

- Have students perform one of the prompts on the spot (impromptu) without time to discuss it.

- During a performance, freeze action, then call additional students up to assume a role in the scenario. This works well when performing students get stuck!

- Allow students to contribute new scenarios and prompts.

DOI: 10.4324/9781003264491-2

## Knowing Yourself Skits

- Pride Example
- Feelings of Inadequacy Example
- Pride
- Feelings of Inadequacy
- Perfectionism
- Self-Confidence
- Asking for Help
- Feeling Different
- Patience
- Accepting Criticism
- Anxiety
- Perseverance
- Self-Criticism
- Responding Appropriately
- Self-Esteem
- Bravery and Courage
- Overcoming Fear
- Honor and Integrity
- Self-Control
- Making Mistakes
- Morality
- Kindness
- Empathy
- Rules
- Respect

DOI: 10.4324/9781003264491-3

## Knowing Yourself Example

### Pride

#### Problem:

You are in the finals of a school spelling bee. You know how to spell the word but you intentionally miss it because you are worried that if you win, your classmates will call you a spelling geek and give you a hard time about it.

#### Solution:

**Friend:** "I know you knew that word. You missed it on purpose didn't you?"
**You:** "It's no big deal. It's just a stupid spelling bee."
**Friend:** "I know you don't really think that."
**You:** "But if I win, some of the kids will make fun of me?"
**Friend:** "It doesn't matter what others think. Your real friends would be proud of you. I would be proud of you."

---

**Final Thought:**

It is always important to do what makes you happy and not worry so much about what others will say.

---

Laurie Stolmack Eaton 2022, *Engaging Social-Emotional Skits for Gifted Students,* by Routledge

# Knowing Yourself Example

## Feelings of Inadequacy

### Problem:

Your friend barely tries something before they quit and say they're no good at it. You want them to come join you in a game of kickball but, as usual, they say no.

### Solution:

**You:** "Do you want to come play kickball with us today at recess?"
**Friend:** "I don't think so. I stink at kickball."
**You:** "You say that about everything. Come on."
**Friend:** "Well, what if I make a fool of myself?"
**You:** "It doesn't matter. The winning team won't be getting a trophy. Just come have fun with us. You won't get better at something unless you put in the time."
**Friend:** "Ok, I'll give it a try."

---

### Final Thought:

Not many people are really good at something the first few times they try it. Go out and take risks. Try something new and don't worry about being "good enough." Just have fun!

---

Laurie Stolmack Eaton 2022, *Engaging Social-Emotional Skits for Gifted Students,* by Routledge

# GIFTED STUDENTS

## Knowing Yourself

### Pride

**Problem:**

You are in the finals of a school spelling bee. You know how to spell the word but you intentionally miss it because you are worried that if you win, your classmates will call you a spelling geek and give you a hard time about it.

**Friend:** "I know you knew that word. You missed it on purpose didn't you?"
**You:** "But if I win, some of the kids will make fun of me!"

### Solution:

_____

_____

_____

_____

_____

_____

_____

_____

_____

**Final Thought:**

_____

_____

_____

# GIFTED STUDENTS

## Knowing Yourself

### Feelings of Inadequacy

### Problem:

Your friend barely tries something before they quit and say they're no good at it. You want them to come join you in a game of kickball but, as usual, they say no.

**You:**     "Do you want to come play kickball with us today at recess?"
**Friend:**  "I don't think so. I stink at kickball."
**You:**     "You say that about everything. Come on."
**Friend:**  "Well, what if I make a fool of myself?"

### Solution:

_____

_____

_____

_____

_____

_____

_____

_____

_____

**Final Thought:**

_____

_____

_____

Laurie Stolmack Eaton 2022, *Engaging Social-Emotional Skits for Gifted Students*, by Routledge

# GIFTED STUDENTS

## Knowing Yourself

### Perfectionism

### Problem:

The student sitting next to you, rarely turns in their work. You know that they are really bright so you are confused.

**You:** "Why didn't you turn in your project?"
**Student:** "I tried to do it but I couldn't get it perfect, so I gave up."

### Solution:

_____

_____

_____

_____

_____

_____

_____

_____

**Final Thought:**

_____

_____

_____

# Knowing Yourself

## Self-Confidence

### Problem:

You and a group of friends are going to audition for the school talent show. One of your friends is trying to back out at the last minute.

**Friend:**   "I just can't do it. What if I mess up? What if everyone laughs at me?"

### Solution:

_____

_____

_____

_____

_____

_____

_____

_____

| Final Thought: |
| --- |
| _____ |
| _____ |
| _____ |

## Knowing Yourself

### Asking for Help

**Problem:**

You're afraid to ask questions when you don't understand something. You think that because you are smart, you shouldn't need any help.

**Teacher:** "Where's your work that I assigned yesterday?"
**You:** "Ummm . . ."
**Teacher:** "What's going on?"

### Solution:

_____

_____

_____

_____

_____

_____

_____

**Final Thought:**

_____

_____

_____

# GIFTED STUDENTS

## Knowing Yourself

### Feeling Different

### Problem:

You notice a student who is always by themselves at lunch and on the playground. One day the teacher asks the two of you to partner up for a project, so you decide to ask them why they choose to be alone.

**You:** "Why are you always by yourself?"
**Student:** "Because I have absolutely nothing in common with the kids in this school."

### Solution:

_____

_____

_____

_____

_____

_____

_____

_____

| Final Thought: |
| --- |
| _____ |
| _____ |
| _____ |

## Knowing Yourself

### Patience

### Problem:

There is a student in your class who is very impatient and always blurts out answers to the teacher's questions without waiting to be called on.

**You:**      "You always blurt out answers and the rest of us don't get a chance to speak."
**Student:**  "I can't help it. It just comes out before I can stop myself."
**You:**      "I have a suggestion."

### Solution:

_____

_____

_____

_____

_____

_____

_____

_____

**Final Thought:**

_____

_____

_____

# GIFTED STUDENTS

## Knowing Yourself

### Accepting Criticism

### Problem:

The teacher told a student that their work was not done correctly and they needed to try again.

**Student:** "That teacher stinks! She said that my work is *terrible*!"
**Friend:** "She didn't say *terrible*. It's just not correct. How can you do a better job accepting criticism of your work?"

### Solution:

_____

_____

_____

_____

_____

_____

_____

_____

_____

| Final Thought: |
| --- |
| _____ |
| _____ |
| _____ |

Laurie Stolmack Eaton 2022, *Engaging Social-Emotional Skits for Gifted Students,* by Routledge

# GIFTED STUDENTS

## Knowing Yourself

### Anxiety

#### Problem:

Your class is heading to the auditorium to see a show. You notice that your friend is looking really anxious and nervous.

**You:** "What's up with you?"

**Friend:** "I really want to see the show but I hate the auditorium. It's too loud and crowded and I don't like when they turn off the lights."

**You:** "I have an idea that is going to help."

### Solution:

_____

_____

_____

_____

_____

_____

_____

_____

_____

**Final Thought:**

_____

_____

_____

## Knowing Yourself

### Perseverance

### Problem:

You are different from many of the other kids at your school. You dress different, your hair is different, and you have unusual interests.

**Student:** "You're so weird! Why do you dress and act like that?"
**You:** "It's what I like. It's who I am."
**Student:** "Well, you should try to fit in."

### Solution:

_____

_____

_____

_____

_____

_____

_____

_____

_____

**Final Thought:**

_____

_____

_____

Laurie Stolmack Eaton 2022, *Engaging Social-Emotional Skits for Gifted Students*, by Routledge

# Knowing Yourself

## Self-Criticism

### Problem:

A student that sits next to you in class always puts themselves down. This bothers you because you know the student is talented.

**Student:** "I am a terrible drawer! I'll never get this to look right!"
**You:** "Why are you always so hard on yourself? I think . . ."

### Solution:

_____

_____

_____

_____

_____

_____

_____

_____

_____

**Final Thought:**

_____

_____

_____

# Knowing Yourself

## Responding Appropriately

### Problem:

The teacher is asking the students to help clean up the classroom at the end of the day.

**Teacher:** "Could everyone stop what they're doing and help us get the room back in order before we leave for the day?"

**Student:** "I didn't make this mess, so I'm not cleaning it up."

### Solution:

_____

_____

_____

_____

_____

_____

_____

_____

_____

_____

**Final Thought:**

_____

_____

_____

## Knowing Yourself

### Self-Esteem

### Problem:

You know a student who complains and criticizes when things don't go their way. They put down others constantly. You're pretty sure this is a case of low self-esteem.

**Student:** "See that girl over there? She got the lead in the school play. I should have gotten the role. She's not even very talented."

### Solution:

_____

_____

_____

_____

_____

_____

_____

_____

| **Final Thought:** |
| --- |
| _____ |
| _____ |
| _____ |

Laurie Stolmack Eaton 2022, *Engaging Social-Emotional Skits for Gifted Students*, by Routledge

# GIFTED STUDENTS

## Knowing Yourself

### Bravery and Courage

### Problem:

Two students are discussing getting up in front of the class to give a presentation. One student admits that they are really scared.

**Student:** "I'm trying to be brave but inside I'm really scared. What should I do?"

### Solution:

_____

_____

_____

_____

_____

_____

_____

_____

---

**Final Thought:**

_____

_____

_____

Laurie Stolmack Eaton 2022, *Engaging Social-Emotional Skits for Gifted Students,* by Routledge

## Knowing Yourself

### Overcoming Fear

**Problem:**

Your friend tells you that they are afraid when they wake up in the middle of the night, so they go to their parents' room to sleep.

**Friend:** "My mom told me that I'm getting too old to come to her room at night, but I get really scared when I wake up and everyone else is asleep."

**You:** "I have an idea that you can try that works for me when this happens."

### Solution:

_____

_____

_____

_____

_____

_____

_____

_____

| **Final Thought:** |
|---|
| _____ |
| _____ |
| _____ |

Laurie Stolmack Eaton 2022, *Engaging Social-Emotional Skits for Gifted Students*, by Routledge

# GIFTED STUDENTS

## Knowing Yourself

### Honor and Integrity

### Problem:

A friend gets a poor grade on a test and they are considering changing the grade before taking it home to their parents.

**Friend:** "I think I can change this grade without my parents noticing."
**You:** "That's dishonest."
**Friend:** "It's no big deal. Who does it hurt?"

### Solution:

_____

_____

_____

_____

_____

_____

_____

_____

_____

| Final Thought: |
| --- |
| _____ |
| _____ |
| _____ |

# GIFTED STUDENTS

## Knowing Yourself

### Self-Control

**Problem:**

During a game, your friend gets angry when an opposing player calls them a hurtful name. It's a good thing that you're there to give your friend some advice so that this situation doesn't get out of hand.

**You:**     "Calm down!"
**Friend:**  "But you heard him, he started it!"

**Solution:**

_____

_____

_____

_____

_____

_____

_____

_____

_____

_____

| **Final Thought:** |
| --- |
| _____ |
| _____ |
| _____ |

Laurie Stolmack Eaton 2022, *Engaging Social-Emotional Skits for Gifted Students*, by Routledge

# Knowing Yourself

## Making Mistakes

### Problem:

The class is building bridges out of toothpicks and you are worried that you will make a mistake, ruin your bridge, and get a bad grade.

**Teacher:**  "Why don't I see you working on your bridge?"
**You:**  "I want to but I'm afraid I'll make a mistake and really mess it up."

### Solution:

_____

_____

_____

_____

_____

_____

_____

_____

**Final Thought:**

_____

_____

_____

## Knowing Yourself

### Morality

**Problem:**

You are in a store with a friend who has no money. While you are paying for your soda, you look over and see your friend steal a candy bar.

**Solution:**

_____

_____

_____

_____

_____

_____

_____

_____

**Final Thought:**

_____

_____

_____

## Knowing Yourself

### Kindness

**Problem:**

You open up a birthday gift from a relative and it is something that you really didn't want.

**Relative:** "I spent a long time looking for the perfect gift for you. I hope you like it."

**Solution:**

_____

_____

_____

_____

_____

_____

_____

_____

_____

**Final Thought:**

_____

_____

_____

# GIFTED STUDENTS

## Knowing Yourself

### Empathy

### Problem:

Your friend tells you that they sometimes feel as though they don't belong. You are concerned because you can relate.

**Friend:** "I feel so different from the other kids. Why can't I just be normal?"
**You:** "I get it. Here's what I do when I feel that way."

### Solution:

_____

_____

_____

_____

_____

_____

_____

_____

_____

**Final Thought:**

_____

_____

_____

Laurie Stolmack Eaton 2022, *Engaging Social-Emotional Skits for Gifted Students,* by Routledge

# GIFTED STUDENTS

## Knowing Yourself

## Rules

### Problem:

It is the first day of school. The teacher tells the class that she is not sure she wants class rules this year. At first you are excited but soon you are confused by this announcement.

**Teacher:** "I'm thinking of having no class rules this year. What do you think?"
**Students:** "YAY!"
**Teacher:** "Really, let's discuss the pros and cons of this idea."

### Solution:

_____

_____

_____

_____

_____

_____

_____

_____

**Final Thought:**

_____

_____

_____

# GIFTED STUDENTS

## Knowing Yourself

### Respect

**Problem:**

Adults are always telling you that you need to be respectful. You're not really sure that you feel this way.

**Mom:**    "It is very important that you show everyone respect."
**You:**      "But what do I do if someone is not being respectful toward me?"

**Solution:**

_____

_____

_____

_____

_____

_____

_____

_____

**Final Thought:** _____

_____

_____

_____

Laurie Stolmack Eaton 2022, *Engaging Social-Emotional Skits for Gifted Students*, by Routledge

## Task Commitment Skits

- Fear of Failure     Example
- Hypersensitive     Example
- Fear of Failure
- Hypersensitive
- Overreacting
- Leadership
- Boredom
- Trouble Focusing
- Taking Responsibility
- Study Skills
- Taking Risks
- Decision Making
- Goal Setting
- Facing Challenges
- Schedule Changes
- Making a Difference

DOI: 10.4324/9781003264491-4

# GIFTED STUDENTS

## Task Commitment Example

### Fear of Failure

#### Problem:

Two students are talking after just finishing a test. One student admits they cheated on the test.

**One:**    "Don't tell, but I was really worried that I wouldn't pass the test so I cheated."
**Two:**    "I can't believe you did that. I studied really hard and you'll probably get a better grade than I got. That's really not fair."
**One:**    "I feel really bad about it. What should I do?"

#### Solution:

**Two:**    "What about speaking to the teacher about it and seeing if she'll let you retake the test."
**One:**    "That's really scary but I'll do it. Thanks."

---

### Final Thought:

Everyone blows it once in a while. Be honest. Even though you may not like the results, you'll still feel better about yourself in the end.

---

Laurie Stolmack Eaton 2022, *Engaging Social-Emotional Skits for Gifted Students*, by Routledge

**ENGAGING SOCIAL-EMOTIONAL SKITS FOR**

# GIFTED STUDENTS

## Task Commitment Example

## Hypersensitive

### Problem:

You are really distracted because students are whispering nearby and the student next to you keeps going to the front of the class to get a tissue. Although it's not a big deal to most people, it makes you lose focus.

**Teacher:** "Why aren't you working?"
**You:** "I can't concentrate."
**Teacher:** "Well, can you think of anything that you can do so that these distractions won't interrupt you?"

### Solution:

**You:** "What about putting in earplugs or wearing headphones when I need to concentrate on my work?"
**Teacher:** "That sounds good as long as you use them only for independent work. Do you have any other ideas?"
**You:** "What if I move to a desk that faces the wall so that I can't see what's going on around me?"

---

**Final Thought:**

Don't just stop working. Instead, find solutions that will work for you. If one thing doesn't work, come up with another option.

---

Laurie Stolmack Eaton 2022, *Engaging Social-Emotional Skits for Gifted Students*, by Routledge

# Task Commitment

## Fear of Failure

### Problem:

Two students are talking after just finishing a test. One student admits they cheated on the test.

**One:** "Don't tell, but I was really worried that I wouldn't pass the test so I cheated."

**Two:** "I can't believe you did that. I studied really hard and you'll probably get a better grade than I got. That's really not fair."

**One:** "I feel really bad about it. What should I do?"

### Solution:

_____

_____

_____

_____

_____

_____

_____

_____

**Final Thought:**

_____

_____

_____

Laurie Stolmack Eaton 2022, *Engaging Social-Emotional Skits for Gifted Students*, by Routledge

# Task Commitment

## Hypersensitive

### Problem:

You are really distracted because students are whispering nearby and the student next to you keeps going to the front of the class to get a tissue. Although it's not a big deal to most people, it makes you lose focus.

**Teacher:** "Why aren't you working?"
**You:** "I can't concentrate."
**Teacher:** "Well, can you think of anything that you can do so that these distractions won't interrupt you?"

### Solution:

_____

_____

_____

_____

_____

_____

_____

_____

_____

_____

| Final Thought: |
| --- |
| _____ |
| _____ |
| _____ |

Laurie Stolmack Eaton 2022, *Engaging Social-Emotional Skits for Gifted Students*, by Routledge

# GIFTED STUDENTS

## Task Commitment

### Overreacting

**Problem:**

The teacher tells the students to line up for lunch and you're the first in line. Another student cuts in front of you.

**Student:** "I wanted to be first in line!"
**You:** "Well, I got here first."
**Student:** "No fair, I wanted to be first in line!"

### Solution:

_____

_____

_____

_____

_____

_____

_____

_____

**Final Thought:**

_____

_____

_____

Laurie Stolmack Eaton 2022, *Engaging Social-Emotional Skits for Gifted Students*, by Routledge

# GIFTED STUDENTS

## Task Commitment

## Leadership

### Problem:

There is a student in your classroom who gets really mad if you don't use all of their ideas when you're working on a project together.

**Student:** "So, I decided what we need to do for our project."
**You:** "Dude, this is a group project so we need to use both of our ideas."
**Student:** "No! I want to use my ideas!"

### Solution:

_____

_____

_____

_____

_____

_____

_____

_____

_____

**Final Thought:**

_____

_____

_____

Laurie Stolmack Eaton 2022, *Engaging Social-Emotional Skits for Gifted Students*, by Routledge

## Task Commitment

### Boredom

### Problem:

Every week the students in your classroom get a spelling worksheet. You don't like doing the same thing for spelling every week so you decide that you will just stop doing it.

**Teacher:** "Why didn't you do your spelling work today?"
**You:** "I don't like doing the same thing for spelling every single week and I always get good grades on my spelling tests. Can I do something different?"
**Teacher:** "What do you suggest?"

### Solution:

_____

_____

_____

_____

_____

_____

_____

_____

**Final Thought:**

_____

_____

_____

Laurie Stolmack Eaton 2022, *Engaging Social-Emotional Skits for Gifted Students,* by Routledge

**ENGAGING SOCIAL-EMOTIONAL SKITS FOR**

# GIFTED STUDENTS

# Task Commitment

## Trouble Focusing

### Problem:

You have trouble focusing and you often forget to do tasks that your teacher assigns during the school day.

**Teacher:** "I think the two of us need to discuss some ways that will help you to stay focused so that you don't miss class work. Do you have any ideas?"

### Solution:

_____

_____

_____

_____

_____

_____

_____

_____

**Final Thought:**

_____

_____

_____

Laurie Stolmack Eaton 2022, *Engaging Social-Emotional Skits for Gifted Students*, by Routledge

# Task Commitment

## Taking Responsibility

### Problem:

Your parent tells you that you are, "*Shirking your responsibilities*."

**Parent:** "Did you do your homework and put your clothes away?"
**You:** "I forgot."
**Parent:** "Listen, you have some jobs to do here at home and they aren't getting done. We need to figure out a solution to this problem. Do you have any ideas?"

### Solution:

_____

_____

_____

_____

_____

_____

_____

_____

**Final Thought:**

_____

_____

_____

Laurie Stolmack Eaton 2022, *Engaging Social-Emotional Skits for Gifted Students*, by Routledge

## Task Commitment

### Study Skills

### Problem:

You have a lot of interests and activities that you like to do after school. Sometimes you get distracted and forget to do your schoolwork.

**Mom:** "I just found out from your teacher that you have several assignments that you didn't turn in. This is getting serious."

**You:** "I know, but I like to get on my computer when I get home and I'm in the middle of a Lego project and I'm hungry when I get home, and . . ."

**Mom:** "Ok, enough! I get it! We need to figure out a solution to this problem. Any ideas?"

### Solution:

_____

_____

_____

_____

_____

_____

_____

_____

| Final Thought: |
| --- |
| _____ |
| _____ |
| _____ |

## Task Commitment

### Taking Risks

### Problem:

You've been putting off learning how to ride a bike because you worry that you won't be able to do it and everyone will laugh at you.

**Friend:** "Hey, do you want to go for a bike ride after school today?"
**You:** "Well, I have to tell you something but please don't tell anyone. I can't ride a bike."

### Solution:

_____

_____

_____

_____

_____

_____

_____

_____

**Final Thought:**

_____

_____

_____

# Task Commitment

## Decision Making

## Problem:

The teacher assigned the students to research and present something on the solar system. On the day the project was due, a student didn't have a project to turn in.

**Teacher:** "Why didn't you turn in your assignment?"
**Student:** "I couldn't decide what to do it on. I like the Milky Way, black holes, space travel . . . I just couldn't choose."
**Teacher:** "You need to be able to make a decision and follow through with it. Let's come up with some ideas so this doesn't happen again."

## Solution:

_____

_____

_____

_____

_____

_____

_____

_____

| Final Thought: |
| --- |
| |
| |
| |

## Task Commitment

### Goal Setting

### Problem:

You have many things that you WANT to do and some things that you NEED to do and it's hard to make it all work.

**Mom:** "You have a lot of home and school responsibilities that you need to get done and it's not happening."

**You:** "But I can't just work, work, WORK. I need time to do what I want to do."

**Mom:** "So let's come up with a solution that we can both live with."

### Solution:

_____

_____

_____

_____

_____

_____

_____

_____

**Final Thought:**

_____

_____

_____

Laurie Stolmack Eaton 2022, *Engaging Social-Emotional Skits for Gifted Students*, by Routledge

# GIFTED STUDENTS

## Task Commitment

### Facing Challenges

### Problem:

The teacher assigned a written report on a specific topic. It's really hard for you to write and you're agitated because the teacher keeps giving writing assignments.

**Teacher:** "What's up? Why aren't you doing your work?"
**You:** "Well, you know that writing is hard for me so . . ."
**Teacher:** "So . . . what?"

### Solution:

_____

_____

_____

_____

_____

_____

_____

_____

_____

**Final Thought:**

_____

_____

_____

Laurie Stolmack Eaton 2022, *Engaging Social-Emotional Skits for Gifted Students*, by Routledge

# GIFTED STUDENTS

## Task Commitment

### Schedule Changes

### Problem:

The teacher sometimes changes the schedule and this really makes you uncomfortable. You like to follow a schedule so that you always know what is coming and what is expected of you.

**You:**     "I'm not comfortable with schedule changes and I was wondering if you could do something so that I know ahead of time that the schedule is going to change?"

**Teacher:**  "Well, what do you suggest?"

### Solution:

_____

_____

_____

_____

_____

_____

_____

_____

_____

| **Final Thought:** |
|---|
| _____ |
| _____ |
| _____ |

Laurie Stolmack Eaton 2022, *Engaging Social-Emotional Skits for Gifted Students*, by Routledge

# Task Commitment

## Making a Difference

### Problem:

A teacher challenges his class to come up with a cause to get behind that will enrich the lives of students at the school (recycling, special club, charity, etc.).

**Friend:** "This is great! Let's team up and come up with something really special."
**You:** "And let's make sure it's something everyone will like."

### Solution:

_____

_____

_____

_____

_____

_____

_____

_____

_____

_____

| Final Thought: |
| --- |
| _____ |
| _____ |
| _____ |

# PEER RELATIONS

## Peer Relations Skits

- Partnership Example
- Fitting In Example
- Partnership
- Fitting In
- Expectations of Others
- Empathy
- Peer Group Rejection
- Commanding
- Cooperation
- Loyalty
- Peer Pressure
- Honesty
- Excessive Competitiveness
- Fair Share
- Easily Upset
- Good Sportsmanship
- Being Alone
- Teasing
- Critical of Others
- Forgiveness
- Understanding Bullies
- Kindness
- Selflessness
- Caring for Others
- Rights and Responsibilities
- Friendship
- Defending a Friend

DOI: 10.4324/9781003264491-5

# GIFTED STUDENTS

# Peer Relations Example

## Partnerships

### Problem:

The teacher asks students to pick a partner for a science experiment. You usually pair up with one particular student but today you would like to pair up with someone else.

**Student:** "I can't believe you aren't working with me! Why are you mad at me?"
**You:** "I'm not mad at you."
**Student:** "Then why won't you work with me?"

### Solution:

**You:** "I know we work well together but I wanted to see what it's like working with someone else. I think that you and I should see how we do, working with other kids. We're just trying something different."
**Student:** "So are we still friends and do you think we can work together on another project sometime?"
**You:** "Definitely!"

---

### Final Thought:

Changing partners can be a great learning experience. Make changing partners something that you and your friend decide together to do so that feelings won't get hurt.

---

Laurie Stolmack Eaton 2022, *Engaging Social-Emotional Skits for Gifted Students*, by Routledge

# GIFTED STUDENTS

## Peer Relations Example

### Fitting In

### Problem:

Your friend has been really down lately. You want to do something or say something that will make them feel better about themselves.

**Friend:** "Why can't I just be like everyone else? I'll never fit in."
**You:** "Why do you want to be like everyone else? I like that you are different."
**Friend:** "But I don't really have many friends."

### Solution:

**You:** "Well, you have me and maybe you can find more friends by getting involved in something you're interested in. That might be a way to find people that are more like you."
**Friend:** "Thanks for making me feel better and giving me ideas to try. You're a good friend."

---

### Final Thought:

It's ok to be different. Try to connect with other people who have the same interests as you and it might very well lead to new friendships.

---

# GIFTED STUDENTS

## Peer Relations

### Partnerships

### Problem:

The teacher asks each student to pick a partner for a science experiment. You usually pair up with one particular student but today you would like to pair up with someone else.

**Student:**  "I can't believe you aren't working with me! Why are you mad at me?"
**You:**  "I'm not mad at you."
**Student:**  "Then why won't you work with me?"

### Solution:

_____

_____

_____

_____

_____

_____

_____

_____

_____

**Final Thought:**

_____

_____

_____

Laurie Stolmack Eaton 2022, *Engaging Social-Emotional Skits for Gifted Students*, by Routledge

# GIFTED STUDENTS

## Peer Relations

### Fitting In

### Problem:

Your friend has been really down lately. You want to do something or say something that will make them feel better about themselves.

**Friend:** "Why can't I just be like everyone else? I'll never fit in."
**You:** "Why do you want to be like everyone else? I like that you are different."
**Friend:** "But I don't really have very many friends."

### Solution:

_____

_____

_____

_____

_____

_____

_____

_____

**Final Thought:**

_____

_____

_____

Laurie Stolmack Eaton 2022, *Engaging Social-Emotional Skits for Gifted Students*, by Routledge

## Peer Relations

## Expectations of Others

### Problem:

A close friend is constantly telling lies. This is really upsetting to you and you decide to confront them and tell them how you feel.

**You:** "Why do you always lie? What's up with that?"
**Friend:** "What do you mean? It's no big deal."

### Solution:

_____

_____

_____

_____

_____

_____

_____

_____

**Final Thought:**

_____

_____

_____

Laurie Stolmack Eaton 2022, *Engaging Social-Emotional Skits for Gifted Students*, by Routledge

# GIFTED STUDENTS

## Peer Relations

### Empathy

**Problem:**

You are out at recess and notice a group of older kids picking on a classmate who is crying and asking for his hat back. You feel really sorry for the classmate so you approach the group.

**Solution:**

_____

_____

_____

_____

_____

_____

_____

_____

**Final Thought:**

_____

_____

_____

Laurie Stolmack Eaton 2022, *Engaging Social-Emotional Skits for Gifted Students*, by Routledge

## ENGAGING SOCIAL-EMOTIONAL SKITS FOR
# GIFTED STUDENTS

# Peer Relations

## Peer Group Rejection

### Problem:

Every day, you sit with the same group of friends in the lunchroom. One day, another classmate approaches the table and sits down.

**Friend:** "You can't sit here! This table is only for us!"

### Solution:

_____

_____

_____

_____

_____

_____

_____

_____

**Final Thought:**

_____

_____

_____

Laurie Stolmack Eaton 2022, *Engaging Social-Emotional Skits for Gifted Students*, by Routledge

# GIFTED STUDENTS

## Peer Relations

### Commanding

### Problem:

A kid is playing with a ball when another kid comes up and takes it.

**Kid One:** "Give me that ball back, booger-head! It's mine!"
**Kid Two:** "It's not your ball."
**Kid One:** "Give it to me!"
**Kid Two:** "I was playing with it. I think I know how we can solve this."

### Solution:

_____

_____

_____

_____

_____

_____

_____

_____

| Final Thought: |
| --- |
| _____ |
| _____ |
| _____ |

# GIFTED STUDENTS

## Peer Relations

## Cooperation

### Problem:

One day, at recess, you and your friend run to the swings. You notice that there is only one swing free.

**You:** "I got here first so I get the swing!"
**Friend:** "I don't want to be your friend anymore!"
**You:** "I have an idea so that we can both swing and it will be fair."

### Solution:

_____

_____

_____

_____

_____

_____

_____

_____

**Final Thought:**

_____

_____

_____

# GIFTED STUDENTS

## Peer Relations

### Loyalty

### Problem:

You are playing a game with a friend when another friend pulls you aside and tells you they have something important to tell you.

**Friend:**    "Don't hang out with him – he's gross."

### Solution:

_____

_____

_____

_____

_____

_____

_____

_____

**Final Thought:**

_____

_____

_____

# GIFTED STUDENTS

## Peer Relations

### Peer Pressure

#### Problem:

A friend approaches you at lunch and asks you to do something that makes you very uncomfortable.

**Friend:** "I'm going to the grocery store after school and I'm going to steel a candy bar. Come with me."
**You:** "I don't know."
**Friend:** "Everybody does it."

#### Solution:

_____

_____

_____

_____

_____

_____

_____

_____

_____

_____

| Final Thought: |
| --- |
| _____ |
| _____ |
| _____ |

# GIFTED STUDENTS

## Peer Relations

### Honesty

### Problem:

Someone in your class asks you to help them with their homework but what they really want to do is copy your work.

**Classmate:** "I really need your help on this homework. Can I see your paper?"

### Solution:

_____

_____

_____

_____

_____

_____

_____

_____

**Final Thought:**

_____

_____

_____

Laurie Stolmack Eaton 2022, *Engaging Social-Emotional Skits for Gifted Students*, by Routledge

# GIFTED STUDENTS

## Peer Relations

### Excessive Competitiveness

### Problem:

You have a friend who is too competitive. They need to be the best at everything and they get really upset when someone does better than them.

**Student:** "You're cheating! I quit, I don't want to play anymore!"
**You:** "I did not cheat! Ok, listen, we need to talk."

### Solution:

_____

_____

_____

_____

_____

_____

_____

_____

_____

**Final Thought:**

_____

_____

_____

Laurie Stolmack Eaton 2022, *Engaging Social-Emotional Skits for Gifted Students,* by Routledge

# GIFTED STUDENTS

## Peer Relations

### Fair Share

**Problem:**

Whenever the teacher puts the students into groups, you tend to end up doing all the work for your group.

**Group Member:** "So, we need to get going on this project. What are *you* going to do?"
**You:** "It's not what *I'm* going to do, it's what *we're* going to do."

**Solution:**

_____

_____

_____

_____

_____

_____

_____

_____

**Final Thought:**

_____

_____

_____

## Peer Relations

### Easily Upset

### Problem:

A student in your class has a hard time working in groups. They cry if the group doesn't use all of their ideas or if someone is working on a part of the project that they wanted to do.

**Student:**   "This isn't fair! I wanted to do that! You're not letting me do anything. I'm telling the teacher!"

### Solution:

_____

_____

_____

_____

_____

_____

_____

_____

_____

**Final Thought:**

_____

_____

_____

Laurie Stolmack Eaton 2022, *Engaging Social-Emotional Skits for Gifted Students*, by Routledge

## Peer Relations

### Good Sportsmanship

### Problem:

You really like to win at games and competitions. Is it worth cheating if it will help you win?

**Friend:**  "I know a way that we can win this game."
**You:**  "Is it against the rules?"
**Friend:**  "Maybe, but we can win!"

### Solution:

_____

_____

_____

_____

_____

_____

_____

_____

**Final Thought:**

_____

_____

_____

ENGAGING SOCIAL-EMOTIONAL SKITS FOR

# GIFTED STUDENTS

## Peer Relations

### Being Alone

### Problem:

Your best friend tells you they want to be alone. You think that they don't want to be your friend.

**You:** "What's wrong? Are you mad at me?"
**Friend:** "I'm not trying to be mean, but I really need to be alone for a while."

### Solution:

_____

_____

_____

_____

_____

_____

_____

_____

_____

| Final Thought: |
| --- |
| _____ |
| _____ |
| _____ |

Laurie Stolmack Eaton 2022, *Engaging Social-Emotional Skits for Gifted Students*, by Routledge

## Peer Relations

### Teasing

**Problem:**

A classmate keeps teasing you and telling lies about you.

**You:** "I've had enough!"
**Friend:** "What are you going to do about it?"

**Solution:**

_____

_____

_____

_____

_____

_____

_____

_____

**Final Thought:**

_____

_____

_____

Laurie Stolmack Eaton 2022, *Engaging Social-Emotional Skits for Gifted Students,* by Routledge

# GIFTED STUDENTS

# Peer Relations

## Critical of Others

### Problem:

A student in your class is always so critical of other students. They always say things like, "Why do you always wear your hair like that?" or "Your handwriting isn't very good."

**You:** "I don't know if you realize it but you're always really critical of others."
**Student:** "What?"
**You:** "You always make comments that aren't very nice. Why is that?"
**Student:** "I'm just telling the truth."

### Solution:

_____

_____

_____

_____

_____

_____

_____

_____

**Final Thought:**

_____

_____

_____

Laurie Stolmack Eaton 2022, *Engaging Social-Emotional Skits for Gifted Students*, by Routledge

## Peer Relations

### Forgiveness

**Problem:**

You lend a friend one of your books. They return it with pages missing.

**You:**    "Hey, what happened to my book? Some of the pages are ripped out!"
**Friend:**  "It was an accident."

**Solution:**

_____

_____

_____

_____

_____

_____

_____

_____

_____

**Final Thought:**

_____

_____

_____

Laurie Stolmack Eaton 2022, *Engaging Social-Emotional Skits for Gifted Students*, by Routledge

# Peer Relations

## Understanding Bullies

### Problem:

Your little brother comes home crying. It turns out that he got beat up by a bunch of kids on the way home from school. You feel really bad for him but you also know that your little brother has a big mouth and always starts fights.

**Little Brother:** "Are you going to help me out, or what?"

### Solution:

_____

_____

_____

_____

_____

_____

_____

_____

_____

_____

**Final Thought:**

_____

_____

_____

Laurie Stolmack Eaton 2022, *Engaging Social-Emotional Skits for Gifted Students,* by Routledge

## Peer Relations

### Kindness

**Problem:**

You offer a student a place to sit on the bus next to you after everyone else refuses.

**Another student:**   "I can't believe you're letting that weirdo sit next to you."

### Solution:

_____

_____

_____

_____

_____

_____

_____

_____

_____

| Final Thought: |
| --- |
| _____ |
| _____ |
| _____ |

# Peer Relations

## Selflessness

### Problem:

A selfless act is doing something for someone else without asking for anything in return.

**Friend:** "There are a lot of people in this school who work really hard and nobody recognizes them for what they do."

**You:** "Let's come up with a way to recognize them."

### Solution:

_____

_____

_____

_____

_____

_____

_____

_____

```
Final Thought:

_____

_____

_____
```

Laurie Stolmack Eaton 2022, *Engaging Social-Emotional Skits for Gifted Students*, by Routledge

## Peer Relations

### Caring for Others

**Problem:**

You always feel really bad when you see someone who is feeling low. You want to do something that will turn their frown upside down.

**You:** "Talia is having a really bad day so I want to come up with something small that will make her feel better."

**Friend:** "I'm in. What can we do?"

### Solution:

_____

_____

_____

_____

_____

_____

_____

_____

**Final Thought:**

_____

_____

_____

Laurie Stolmack Eaton 2022, *Engaging Social-Emotional Skits for Gifted Students*, by Routledge

# GIFTED STUDENTS

# Peer Relations

## Rights and Responsibilities

### Problem:

A kid stole something of yours and then said they'd hurt you if you told on them.

**Friend:** "I saw what just happened. What are you going to do?"

### Solution:

_____

_____

_____

_____

_____

_____

_____

_____

_____

**Final Thought:**

_____

_____

_____

Laurie Stolmack Eaton 2022, *Engaging Social-Emotional Skits for Gifted Students,* by Routledge

## ENGAGING SOCIAL-EMOTIONAL SKITS FOR
# GIFTED STUDENTS

## Peer Relations

### Friendship

**Problem:**

Your class is having a discussion about friendship.

**Teacher:** "I want to know the difference between a friend and a *good* friend."

**Solution:**

_____

_____

_____

_____

_____

_____

_____

_____

**Final Thought:**

_____

_____

_____

# GIFTED STUDENTS

## Peer Relations

### Defending a Friend

### Problem:

Many of the kids in your class are teasing and picking on your best friend. You fear that if you stay friends, everyone will start picking on you, too.

### Solution:

_____

_____

_____

_____

_____

_____

_____

_____

_____

_____

---

**Final Thought:**

_____

_____

_____

---

Laurie Stolmack Eaton 2022, *Engaging Social-Emotional Skits for Gifted Students*, by Routledge